A story about

Wandering

WONDERING

Written by
Melissa Monroe

Illustrated by
Daria Rosso

To the child in all of us
who wonders why

May you find the WONDER in Him
and know He is nearby

That they should seek God,
and perhaps feel their way toward Him
and find Him.
Yet He is actually not far
from each one of us
Acts 17:27

4

Why is this happening? I said with a sigh
Why? Why?
I need to know WHY

Little Lou wandered and wandered; looked and looked
Lou needed to understand
Lou thought and was hooked

Looking into the night sky,
it was empty and dark

wandering through the desert,
the harsh sun made a mark

Crossing the ocean,
getting tossed to and fro

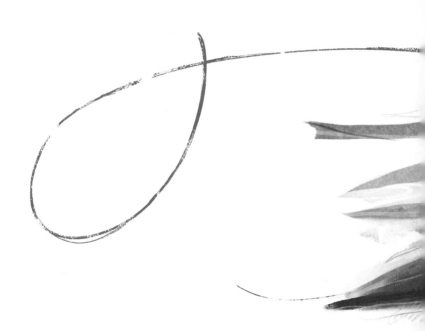

Climbing the mountain,
breathless and low

14

Hiking the long treks,
never reaching the end

Searching under all the rocks,
around every bend

Walking through the fields,
with feet so sore

All this searching became such a chore

Little Lou was tired
and needed to rest

An old friend came along,
and this news was the best

The old friend had
searched and searched,
seeking to understand WHY

Instead of the answer,
beautiful things
came to the eye

Blessings and hard things
together like glue

They happen at the same time
This is so very true

Little Lou thought
and remembered the path

The night sky had
So many stars
So vast

The desert was warm

The sun lit my face

Cool nights refreshed me

I enjoyed the space

The ocean was blue
So dense
So deep
Life teeming below
The surface asleep

Yet movement not still
It carried me through
At times gently
and at times roughly too

The mountain climb was long
So hard I knew

But the reward at the top
was a spectacular view

The hiking treks winded
through so many miles

The path pretty flowers
Their smell brought my smiles

The rocks were abundant
Under each one revealed truth

Seeing this much
makes me happy... it's true

The fields had tall grasses
Dancing carefree in the wind
Never worrying
Never toiling
Seeing how they bend

We are all on a journey
Parts we don't want and sigh
But don't spend all your time
wondering why

See the WONDER in each day
This will lift you high

41

All your wandering and looking
All your seeking to search
Does not solve the mystery
So look over the perch

It points you to Him
Our loving God so true
You're the apple of His eye
He is saying to you

He is in every detail
He is everywhere all around

In the good and the hard
It is there He is found

Beauty is everywhere
for you to see

Look around and sit
Enjoy under this tree

Rest Little Lou
and just let yourself be

You are never alone
That's His promise to you

Walk with Him
hand in hand
and see His love too

This story is born out of adversity.
Melissa's life took a turn as she walked through
a long season of difficulty, loss, and illness.
She had a desperate need to understand why.
But as she came to see, God tenderly and lovingly comforted
her not by answering her question, but by showing her He
is nearer and bigger than any hardship she faced.
This is the story that led to her gift of deepening faith.

Wondering Why seeks to help anyone struggling through
a difficult trial and trying to make sense of it all.
This is for the child in all of us looking for answers.

Melissa Monroe is a designer, entrepreneur, and the author of multiple children's books. As an interior designer for private aircraft, her design practice allows her creativity to flourish. Always dreaming and designing, new ideas were born along the way. She launched a new business and began writing books. Her passion for storytelling and creating experiential environments is the common thread running through all her endeavors. She is honored to share her heart with you.

Daria Rosso was born and raised in Italy. Currently living in London, she has the privilege of being an itinerant artist and illustrator. Art is a way of life for her— the filter through which she perceives the world and shapes it, making it her own. Her style is inspired by traditional scientific illustration, pop art, and photography. The result is artwork with a bright and modern aesthetic, emphasizing realism, color, and bold, spaceless composition. Wondering Why is her debut illustrated book.

Solving why is not our peace
Rest and know your struggle can cease
The answer is found in this simple truth
God says SEEK ME instead of the sleuth

WestBow Press books may be ordered through booksellers or by contacting:

WestBow Press
A Division of Thomas Nelson & Zondervan
1663 Liberty Drive
Bloomington, IN 47403
www.westbowpress.com
844-714-3454

Cover & Interior Illustration Credit: Daria Rosso

ISBN: 978-1-6642-8739-6 (sc)
ISBN: 978-1-6642-8741-9 (hc)
ISBN: 978-1-6642-8740-2 (e)

Library of Congress Control Number: 2022923630

Print information available on the last page.

WestBow Press rev. date: 02/27/2023

WestBow
PRESS®
A DIVISION OF THOMAS NELSON
& ZONDERVAN

In your search for WHY

You find WHO